Christmas!

WE REMEMBER,

REJOICE,

WORSHIP

Created by Mike Speck

Arranged by Mike Speck and Tim Parton

MIKE SPECK
M U S I C

lillenas

lillenas.com

Contents

Celebrate, Rejoice

includes
Celebrate
Rejoice
O Come, O Come, Emmanuel

*Arr. by Mike Speck
and Tim Parton*

PLEASE NOTE: The copying of this music is prohibited by law and is not covered by CCLI or OneLicense.net.

Let's cel - e - brate.____ Let us re -

- joice,____ let's cel - e - brate;____

for the Sav - ior of the____ world is born____ to - day.____

*"Rejoice"

For un-to you, this day,

in the ci - ty of Ju - dah, is born

a Sav - ior which is Christ, the Lord.

*"O Come, O Come, Emmanuel"

- ior of the world is born to-day.

The A-noint - ed One is to be praised.

Sing Hal - le - lu - jah!

108
Let's cel - e - brate.
TENORS only
Re - joice!
Let's cel - e - brate!
C 7 sus
N.C.
F/A
E♭/B♭
B♭
N.C.
111
Stop Claps
Re - joice!
TENORS only
Let's cel - e - brate!
Re - joice!
Re - joice!
F/A
E♭/B♭
B♭
E♭/B♭
B♭
N.C.
F/A
B♭
molto rit.
114
Let's cel - e - brate!
Re - joice!
N.C.
B♭/C
F
molto rit.

Sing a Song of Christmas

with
Joy to the World
Good Christian Men, Rejoice
God Rest Ye Merry, Gentlemen
Hark! the Herald Angels Sing
Angels We Have Heard on High
Birthday of a King

Words and Music by
MARTY FUNDERBURK and DOUG LITTLE
Arr. by Mike Speck and Tim Parton

NARRATOR: It's time to rejoice! *(Music begins)* It's time to embrace the infectious joy that happens this time of year. So let the celebration begin. Let the musicians play. Let the singers sing!

Lift your voice in cel - e - bra - tion, Sing a song of

Christ - mas, sing!

NARRATOR: There is nothing that puts us into the
Christmas spirit quicker than singing our favorite carols.
Stand and join us. Let's all sing the songs of Christmas.

*Start for "Traditional Carol Medley"

*"Joy to the World"

20

CD: 10 | Tempo I ♩. = ca. 84

peat,___ re - peat___ the sound - ing joy.

Tempo I ♩. = ca. 84

D D/F♯ G D Em7 D/F♯ G D/A A D DM7/C♯

f

Good
f

*"Good Christian Men, Rejoice"

Christ - ian men, re - joice___ With heart and soul and

F F/E F/D F/E F F/E

CD: 11

*"God Rest Ye Merry, Gentlemen"

108

Hark! the her - ald an - gels sing, "Glo - ry____ to the

new - born King!

CD: 13

*"Angels We Have Heard on High"

114

An - gels we have heard on high, Sweet - ly sing - ing

CD: 14

*End of "Traditional Carol Medley"

What a Glorious Night
(Solo with Children's Choir)

Words and Music by
BEN MCDONALD, CASEY BROWN,
DAVID FREY and JONATHAN SMITH
Arr. by Mike Speck and Tim Parton

(As previous song ends, Children's Choir enters)

Acoustic feel ♩ = ca. 105

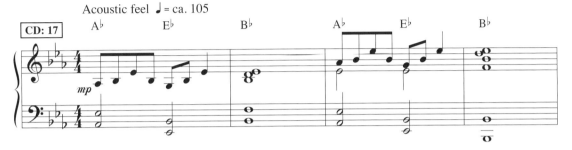

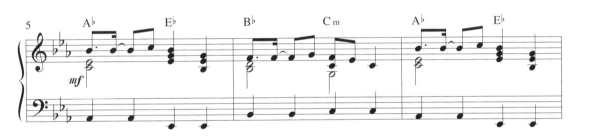

CHILDREN'S CHOIR

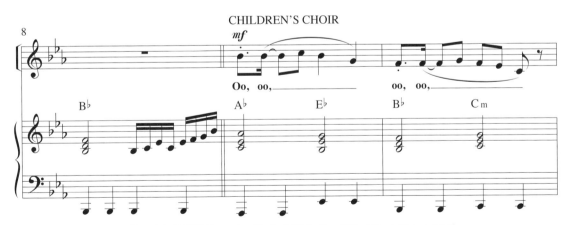

Oo, oo,_____ oo, oo,_____

38

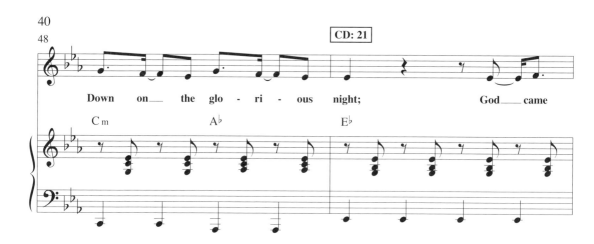

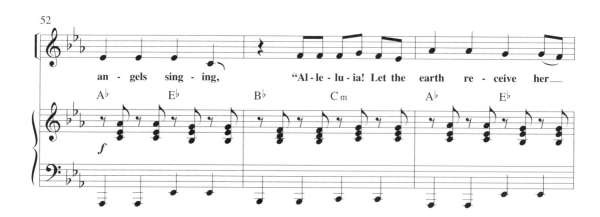

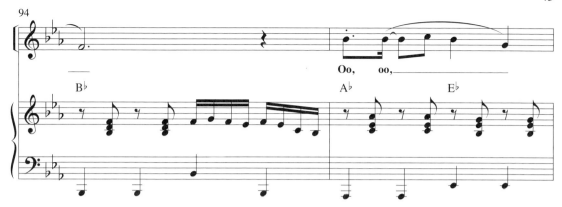

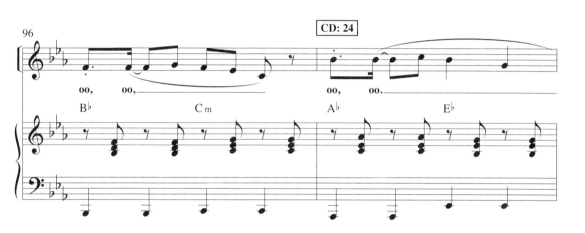

When Love Was Born
(Underscore)

Music by BERNIE HERMS,
STEPHANIE LEWIS and MARK SCHULTZ
Arr. by Mike Speckand Tim Parton

NARRATOR: *(Music begins)* It was a glorious night— a night that would change everything. I want to ask you to let your imagination wander back to a simpler time in history. Before electricity or running water. Long before there were automobiles, telephones, or computers. Picture a tiny village. It's nighttime, and the air is cold and damp. A young man and his teenage wife have walked some seventy miles to reach this small village. Tired and weary, they are in need of a place to stay for the evening. But when they reach the town, it is already overrun with travelers. Every room has been taken. Can you see them as they stand outside the innkeeper's door? The young girl is very close to giving birth to her first child. She's needing a place of warmth. A safe place to sleep. A stable, where animals are sheltered, ends up being the only place offered to them. I can see the young man gathering hay to create a makeshift bed for his precious bride— when suddenly, it is time for her baby to be born!

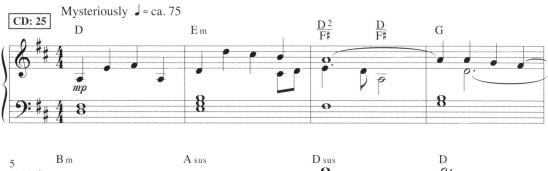

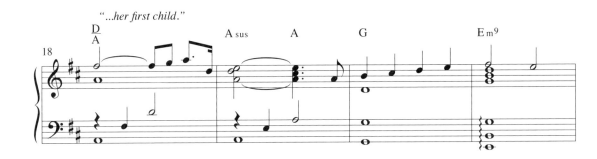

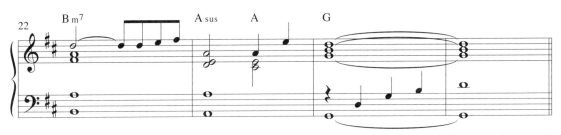

Segue to "When Love Was Born"

When Love Was Born

Words and Music by
BERNIE HERMS, STEPHANIE LEWIS
and MARK SCHULTZ
*Arr. by Mike Speck
and Tim Parton*

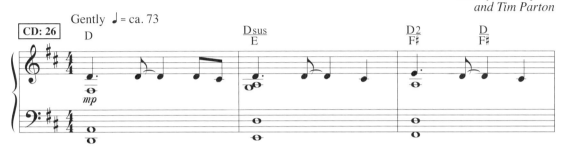

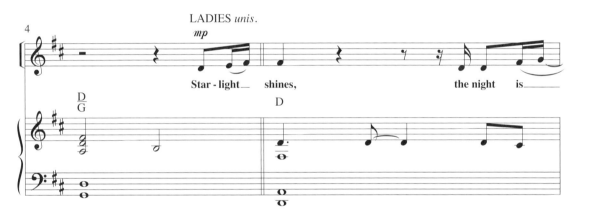

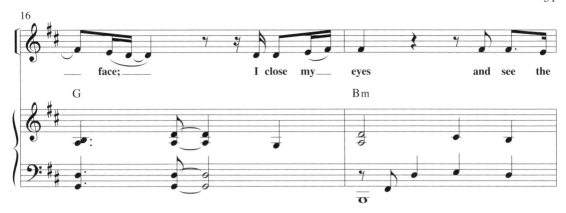

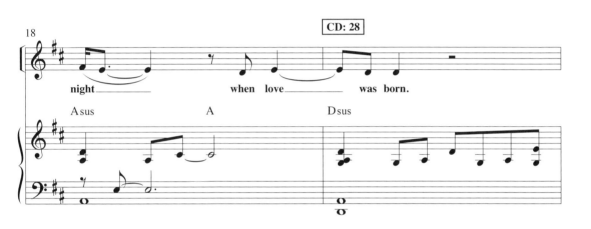

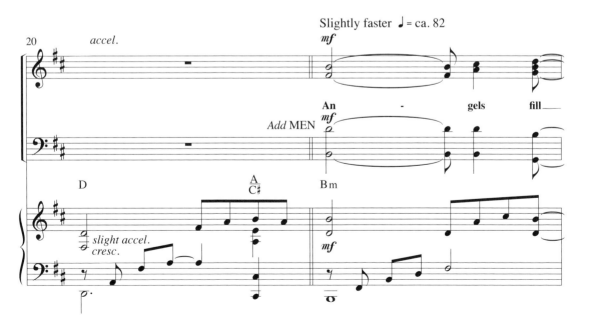

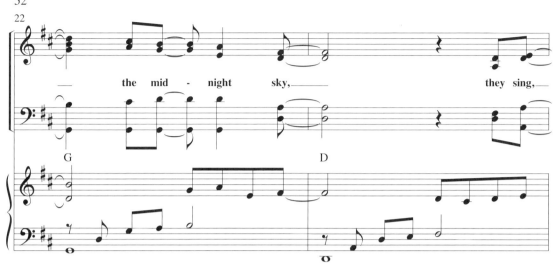

the mid - night sky,___ they sing,___

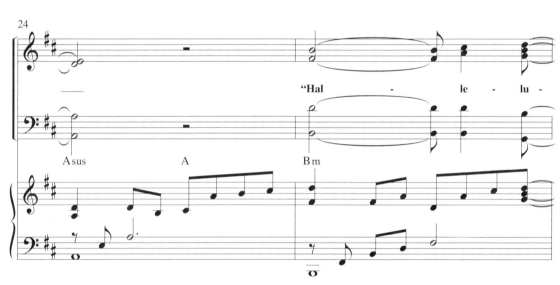

___ "Hal - le - lu -

- ia! He___ is Christ___ our King."___

poco rit.

54

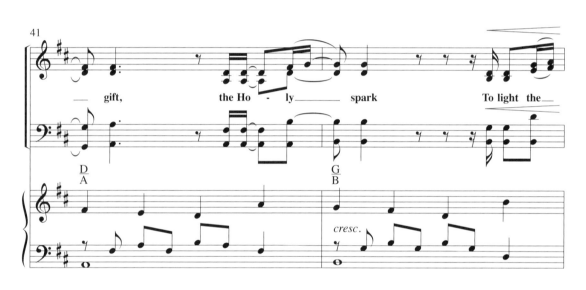

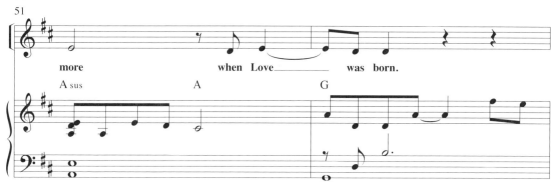

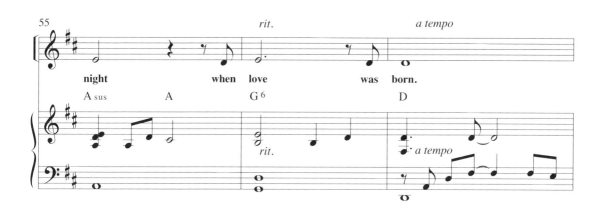

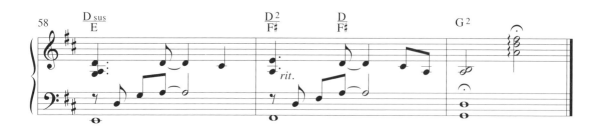

He Came All This Way

Words and Music by
MARK CONDON
Arr. by Mike Speck
and Tim Pardon

NARRATOR: *(Music begins)* Yes, love was born in Bethlehem. Love like mankind had never known. Love that would soon transform the world. On the night that Jesus was born, there were very few who knew his true identity. Mary, Joseph, a band of shepherds . . . a very small group of people, yet all of the inhabitants of heaven knew exactly who He was, and soon the world would realize who that manger really held.

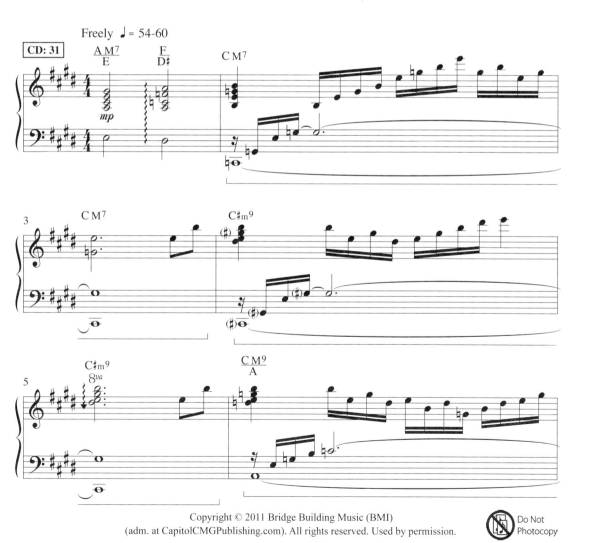

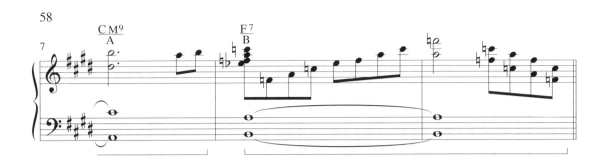

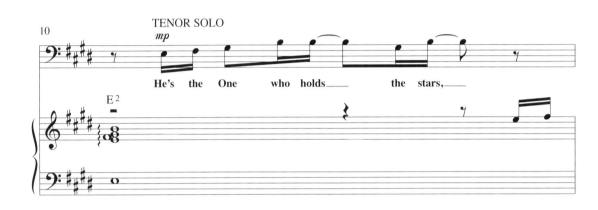

TENOR SOLO

mp

He's the One who holds___ the stars,___

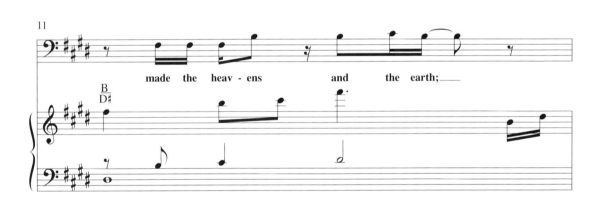

made the heav - ens and the earth;___

He made the day a thou - sand years,___

62

CD: 33

TRIO

66

68

He Has Come

Words and Music by
JASON WHITE
Arr. by Mike Speck
and Tim Parton

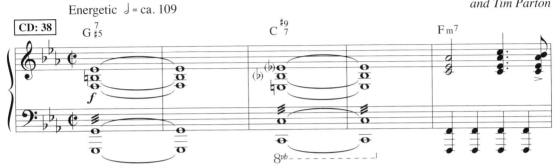

Joy to the world! the Lord is come;

Do Not
Photocopy

74

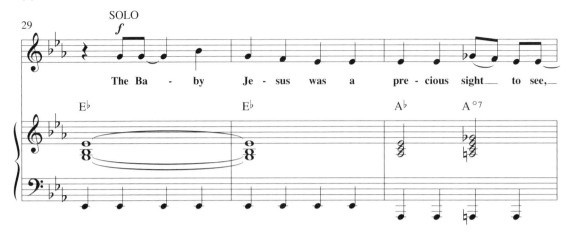

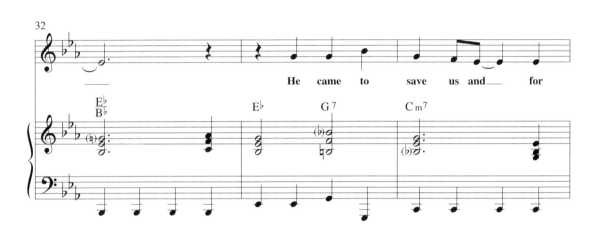

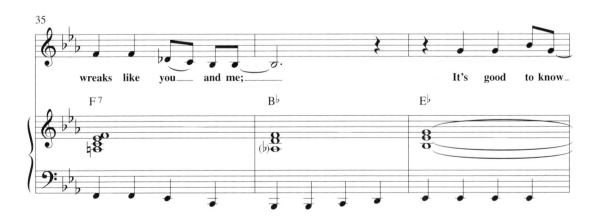

76

CD: 43

Joy, joy, joy! He's come to

bring us joy! Joy, joy, joy!

Opt. 8vb

82

84

139

142

(Without music)

NARRATOR: "For unto us a child is born, unto us a son is given: and the government shall be upon his shoulder: and his name shall be called Wonderful, Counselor, the mighty God, the everlasting Father, the Prince of Peace." So many names attributed to this Child born in Bethlehem. *(Music begins)* But Mary and Joseph are not instructed to call this holy Child by any of these majestic names. The angel of the Lord was very clear as to the earthly name this infant King should be called.

King Jesus Is His Name

with

What Child Is This?

Words and Music by
BABBIE MASON and
DONNA DOUGLAS
Arr. by Mike Speck
and Tim Parton

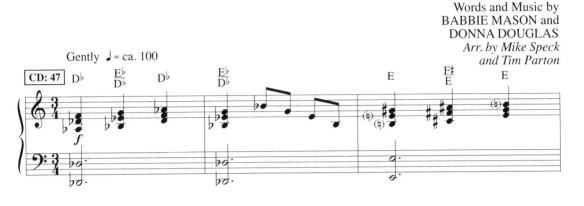

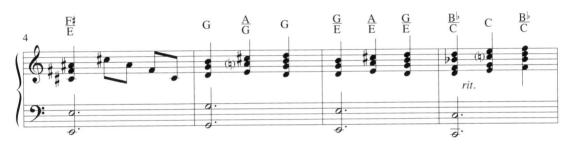

*Words by WILLIAM C. DIX; Music: Traditional English Melody. Arr. © 2016 PsalmSinger Music/BMI (admin. by Music Services). All rights reserved.

King,_____ Whom shep - herds guard_____ and an - gels

sing;_____ Haste, haste____ to bring Him

laud, The Babe,_____ the Son____ of Mar - y.

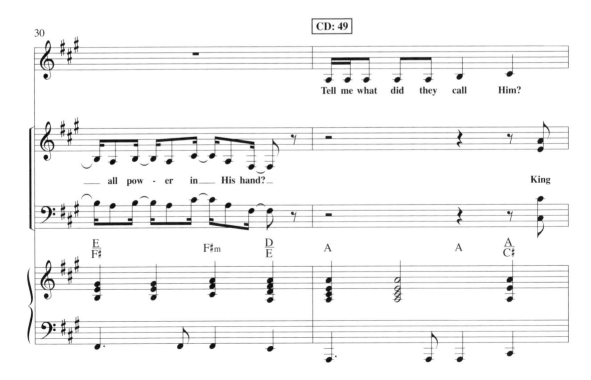

92

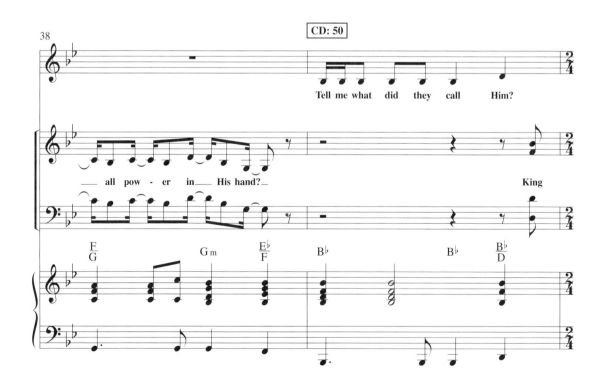

CD: 51

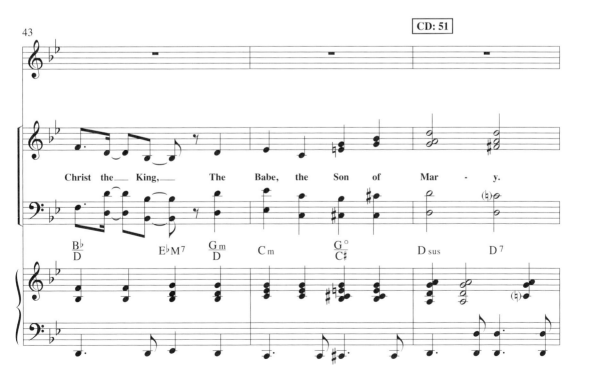

94

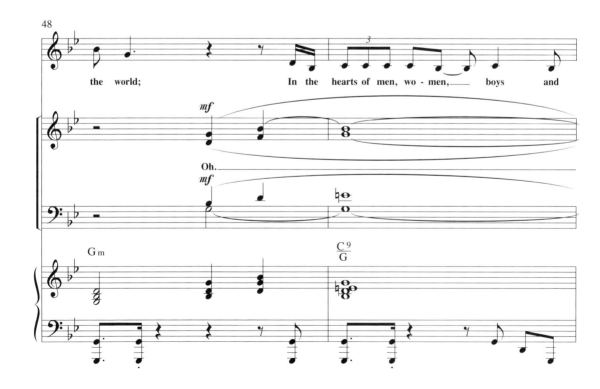

SOLO

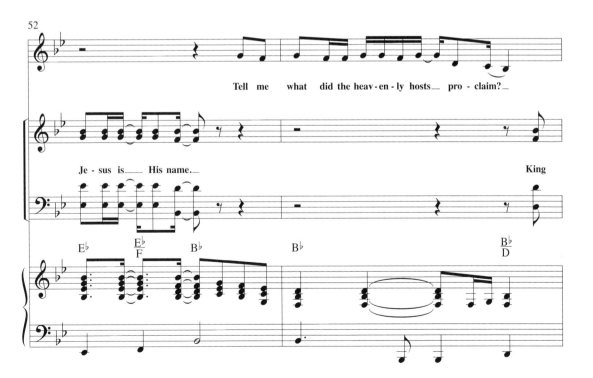

tell me what did the heav-en-ly hosts__ pro - claim?__

Je - sus is__ His name.__

King

Oo, who__ would have tho't__ this ti - ny lad Would hold__

Je - sus is__ His name.

Who__ would have tho't__ this ti - ny lad would hold__

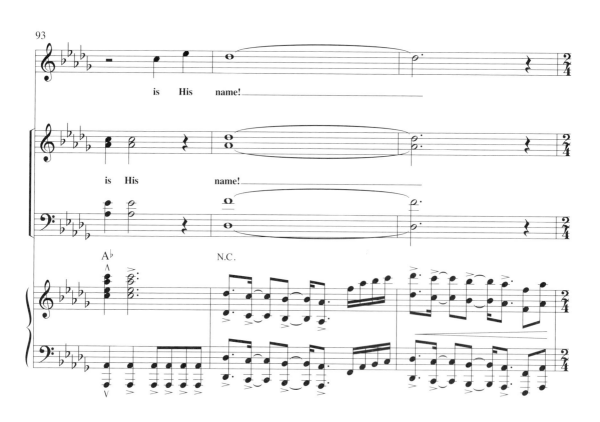

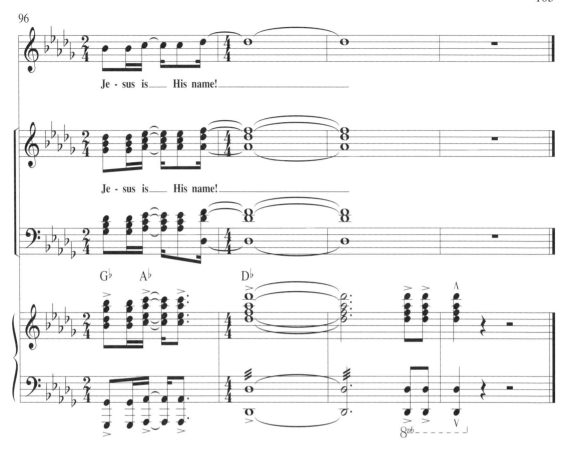

(Without music)

NARRATOR: In recent days, many have tried to reduce this
sacred and blessed event we know as Christmas to a mere
holiday for lavishing gifts on one another and on ourselves.
But Christmas is not just another vacation day on the
calendar. The birth of Jesus Christ, God's only begotten Son,
makes Christmas a holy day. A day for celebrating and
rejoicing, for sure! *(Music begins)* But also a day of solemn
worship and humble thanksgiving. A time for us to give
honor and praise to the One who came to save us from our sin.

A Holy Day

Words and Music by
JEFF BUMGARDNER
and CLIFF DUREN
Arr. by Mike Speck
and Tim Parton

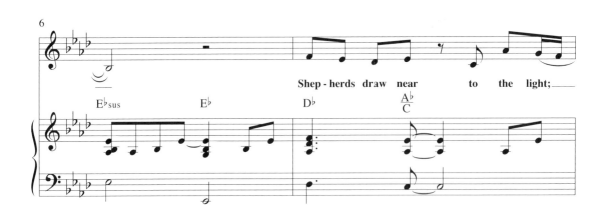

Do Not
Photocopy

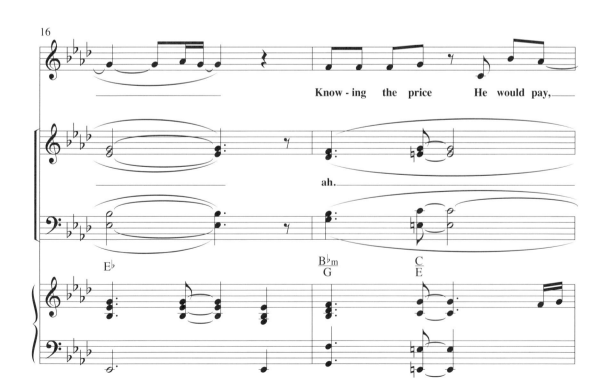

CD: 57

our God is with us; Let all that is in us praise His

our God is with us; Let all that is in us praise His

ho - ly name.

ho - ly name.

31
mf
Sweet hymns of joy we will sing,
mf
Sweet hymns of joy we will sing,
TENORS only mf
D♭
A♭/C
E♭sus
E♭
mf
33
This grate - ful cho - rus we bring;
This grate - ful cho - rus we bring;
D♭
A♭/C
E♭

Chains will be bro - ken, eyes will be o - pened; The

prom - ised Mes - si - ah is mak - ing a way.___

116

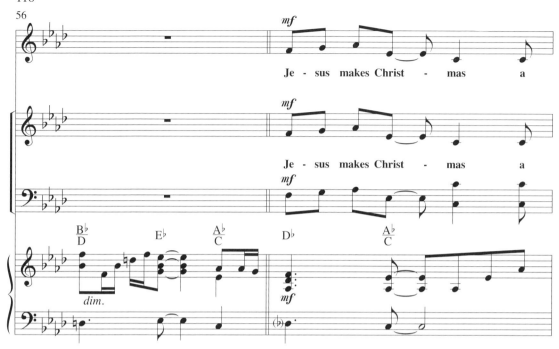

60

we cel - e - brate;_____ Let ev - 'ry na - tion and

cel - e - brate;_____ Let ev - 'ry na - tion and

62

tongue pro - claim,_____ Je - sus makes Christ - mas,

tongue pro - claim,_____ Je - sus makes Christ - mas,

Christmas Worship Medley

includes
O Come, All Ye Faithful
Here I Am to Worship
Holy, Holy, Holy! Lord God Almighty
Revelation Song

*Arr. by Mike Speck
and Tim Parton*

NARRATOR: *(Music begins)* I want to ask everyone in this room to stand.
For a few moments, let's truly worship and adore our Lord and our King.

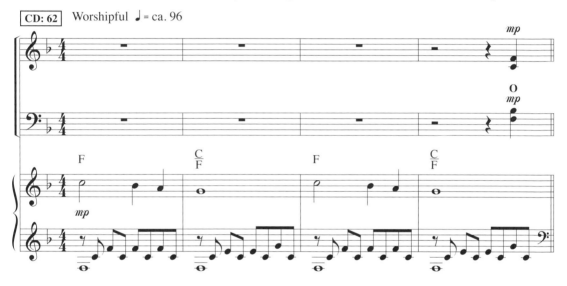

124

*"Here I Am to Worship"

Slightly slower ♩ = ca. 75

worthy, Al - to - geth - er won - der - ful to me.

Here I am to wor - ship, Here I am to

bow down, Here I am to say that You're my God.

128

130

Who was___ and is___ and is___ to come;___

With all cre-a - tion I___ sing. Praise to the King of kings;___

You are my ev-'ry-thing and I will a-dore You.___

You are my ev-'ry-thing and I will a-dore You.

O come, let us a-

dore Him! O come, let us a-

134

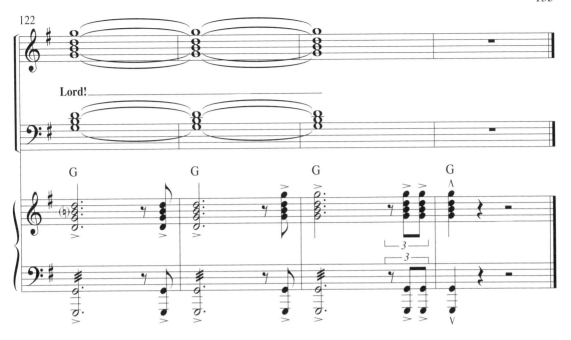

(Without music)

NARRATOR: Christmas truly is the most wonderful time of the year. The very thought of it stirs up all kinds of feelings and emotions. A part of each and every Christmas are the memories we hold precious and dear. But more valuable than those sweet moments is the remembrance of a Savior, who came from heaven and changed the world.

As we retell the story of the birth of Jesus, we are reminded of the angels who proclaimed glad tidings of great joy. We remember Mary and Joseph as they sought for shelter in Bethlehem. Shepherds, wise men, Simeon, King Herod . . . all characters who took part in the wondrous event we call Christmas.

In the midst of remembering that glorious night of miracles, we cannot keep from rejoicing, for we have good reason to rejoice! Jesus Christ, God's Son, came seeking for you and me. He came to love, heal, and forgive! And once you experience his love, his healing, his forgiveness, you cannot keep from praising him and giving him glory.

Bethlehem Morning

(Underscore)

Music by
MORRIS CHAPMAN
Arr. by Mike Speck
and Tim Parton

NARRATOR: *(Music begins)* Christmas is a time of remembering and rejoicing, but most important of all, it's a time to worship; a time to adore the One who came to save us. Looking back at the Christmas story, we find that every person who encountered this holy child worshiped him. We are in good company when we blend our hearts together in worship at Christmas, for we find ourselves in the throngs of the angels and the shepherds and the wise men, who all praised and worshiped this child named Jesus.

And you know the story of Christmas is still being written. For when we bow our knee before the Lord and receive him as our personal Savior, we become a part of the Christmas story. It becomes more than just a memory. It becomes the constant reminder that we have been forgiven of our sins and have received the gift of Christmas, which is eternal life. We no longer simply remember him because now we know him, not just as a babe in Bethlehem but as our Savior and our Lord.

And to think that any day now, this King, the one who was born in Bethlehem, the one who died for us and rose from the dead, will leave his heavenly throne one more time. King Jesus will come to take his children home to live with him in his house forever and ever. And until that moment, we will remember. We will rejoice. And yes, we will worship!

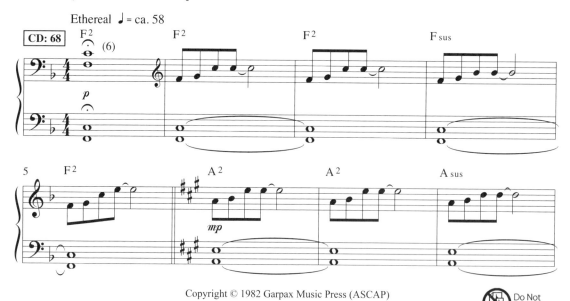

"For when we bow..."

"And to think that..."

Segue to "Bethlehem Morning"

Bethlehem Morning

Words and Music by
MORRIS CHAPMAN
Arr. by Mike Speck and Tim Parton

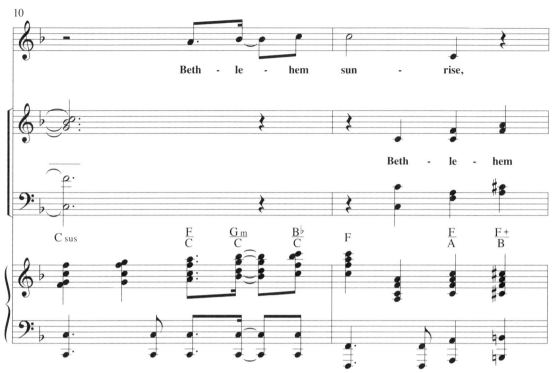

For the Child____ that was born_____ there

eyes;_____

Ah.

His spir-it nev-er dies.

Peace on earth, good -

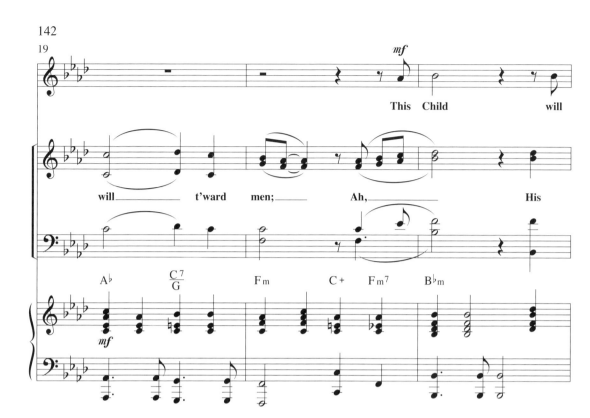

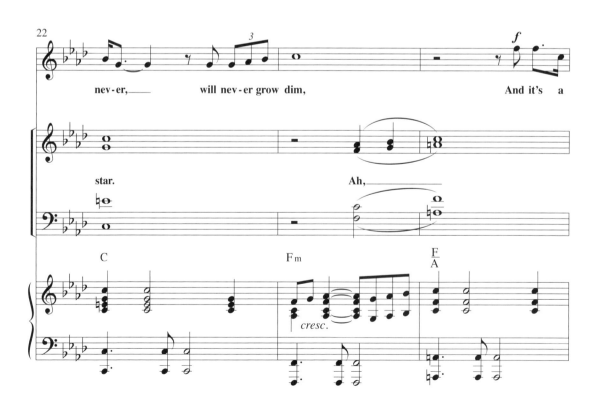

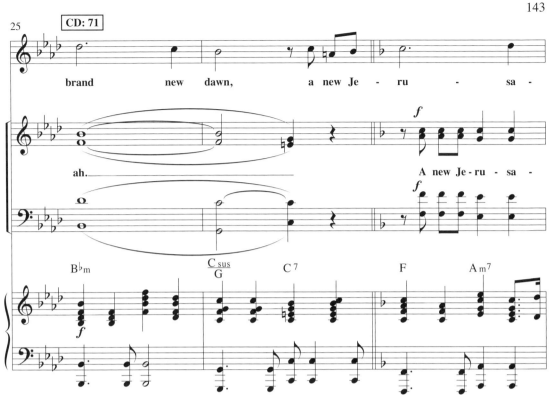

144

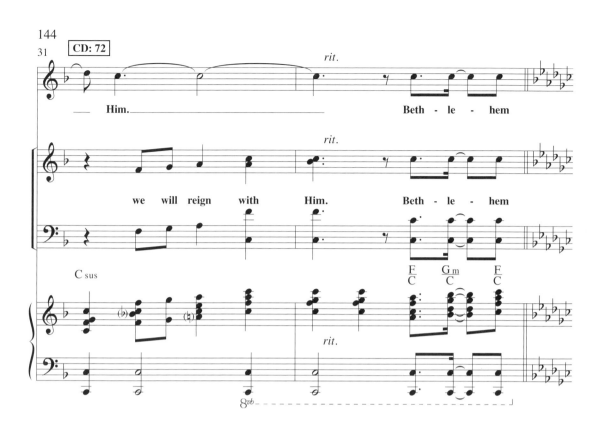

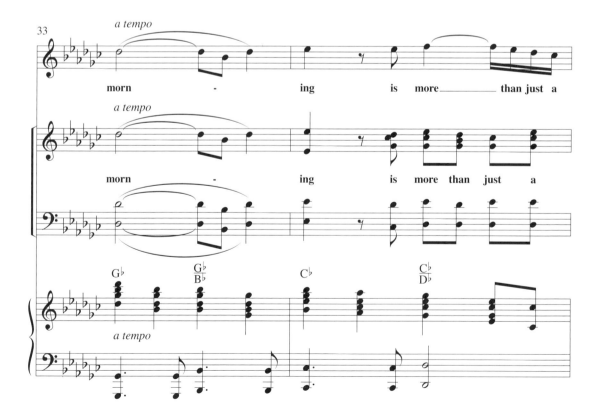

146

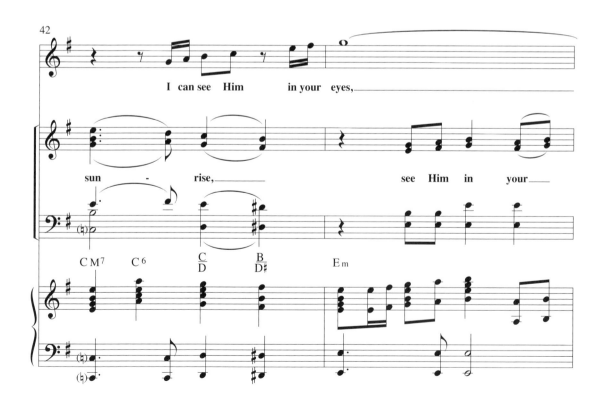

From Bethlehem to Calvary

Words and Music by
RAY (CHIP) DAVIS
Arr. by Mike Speck
and Tim Parton

You al-ways look for a rhyme or a rea-son, You don't know if you be-lieve in the sea - son,

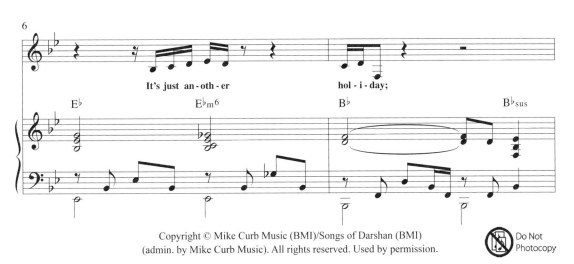

It's just an-oth-er hol-i-day;

Who is this Babe that we give a-dor-a-tion, He is the Sav-ior, the Lord of sal-va - tion,

He is still the same to - day. And

CHOIR

And

16

heart. From His Fa - ther's throne___ in glo - ry, To a

Oo,___ ah,_____ To a

F sus   F   B♭   A♭/C   B♭/D

18

man - ger filled with hay; From Beth - le - hem___ to Cal - va - ry,___

man - ger filled with hay;___ From Beth - le - hem___ to Cal - va - ry,___

E♭   B♭/D   C⁷sus   C⁷   Cm⁷   B♭/D   E♭

fear and the feel-ings you're lock-ing in-side;____ Must you keep it all with-

in? Here is a Man Who al-read-y for-gave you,

CD: 77

He has the pow-er to con-quer and save__ you, If you will on-ly let Him

Note to Ministers of Music: When the congregation takes part in our choral presentations, we engage them at another level. I have placed two songs in this project that are designed to involve the whole congregation. I also wanted to make each of the congregational medleys accessible for use outside the confines of this presentation. In order to make the carols in "Sing a Song of Christmas" work as a standalone worship set, I have placed a CD rehearsal point at the beginning of the carol portion of the medley. We have also noted, for instrumentalists, where the intro should start (when desiring to use the carols portion only).

I have given at least three options for the ending of this musical. Some will want to finish on the song "Bethlehem Morning" and dismiss. For those who choose to have an altar call or time of invitation, the final song, "From Bethlehem to Calvary," will serve as a perfect moment to prepare the pastor for extending an invitation for a time of commitment. Finally, some churches may choose to take a moment to thank the choir, children's choir, musicians, etc., immediately following "Bethlehem Morning" and then use "From Bethlehem to Calvary" as a final song to share before dismissing.

Acknowledgments: I have not been alone in the process of creating this choral book. Thank you to Faye and Melody for all the time they have given to this project. Thanks to Tim Parton for co-arranging this book with me. Thanks, Danny Crawford, for helping me build the tempo maps for the two congregational medleys. Special thanks to Joey Nicholson for the hours you have put into this project. Thank you, Beth Regans, my personal assistant, for your constant support and tireless work. I am grateful to my friend Bruce Cokeroft, who continues to be a source of encouragement and help in so many ways, especially in helping to shape the narration. Thank you to Professor Linda Nell Cooper of Liberty University and her assistance in writing the narration. I appreciate Jim Symons for his friendship and constructive input. To the Indian Trail choir, thank you for singing on this project and making it real. To the children of First Baptist, Indian Trail, and Jonathan Schallmo, I am proud of you and thankful for you. Finally, I want to thank Lillenas Music for this great opportunity to create a tool I can use this coming Christmas. Yippee, my search for Christmas music is over for this year! Hallelujah! Glory to God! (Pinch me; I cannot believe it's possible!)